Richard Le Gallienne

The religion of a literary man

Richard Le Gallienne

The religion of a literary man

ISBN/EAN: 9783337260934

Printed in Europe, USA, Canada, Australia, Japan

Cover: Foto ©Lupo / pixelio.de

More available books at **www.hansebooks.com**

The Religion of
a Literary Man

' The old gods pass'—the cry goes round,
' Lo ! how their temples strew the ground' ;
Nor mark we where, on new-fledged wings,
Faith, like the phænix, soars and sings.

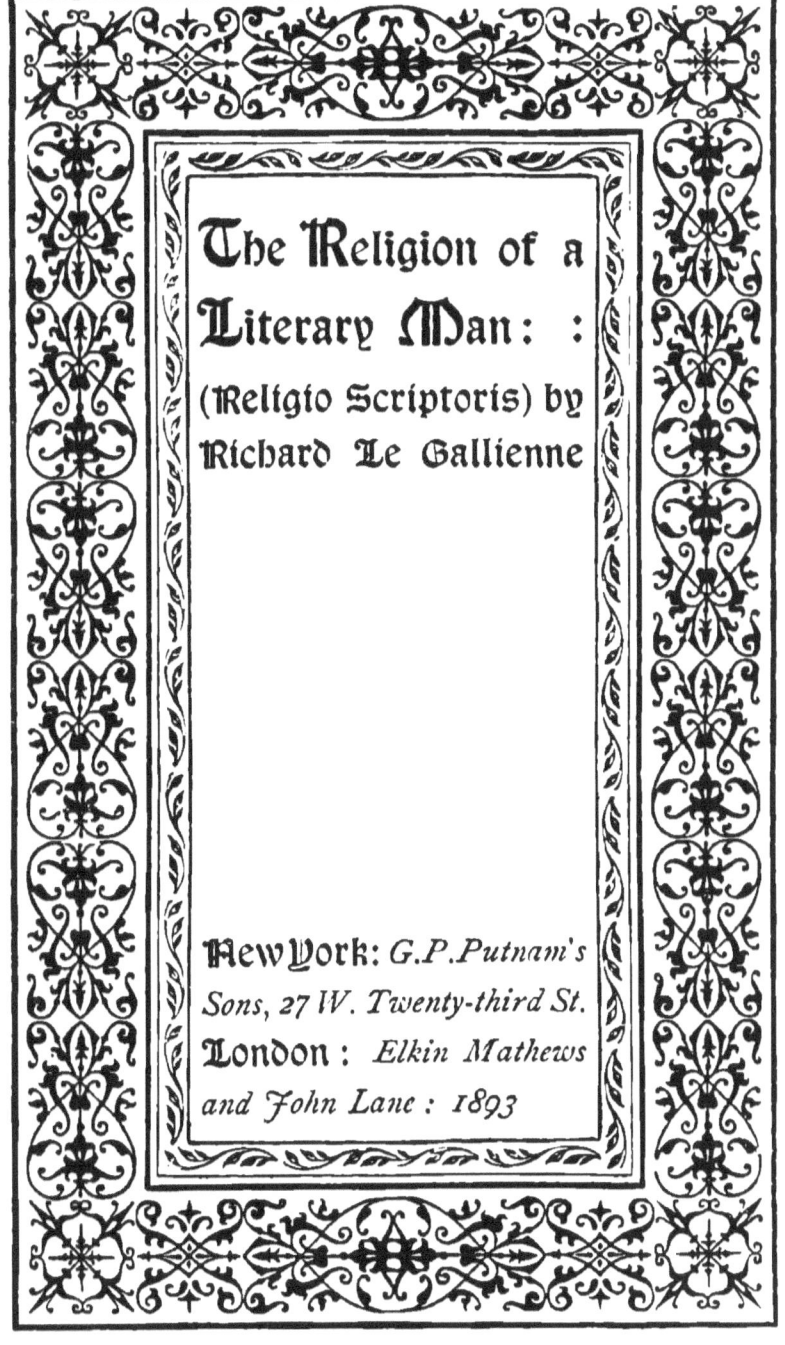

The Religion of a Literary Man: :

(Religio Scriptoris) by
Richard Le Gallienne

New York: *G. P. Putnam's Sons, 27 W. Twenty-third St.* London : *Elkin Mathews and John Lane : 1893*

To A. E. FLETCHER, Esq.

M *Y dear Mr. Fletcher,—Some one has said that the true pulpit of these latter days is the newspaper press. You have been one of the first journalists to apply this dictum. You have realised that even poor 'average humanity' cares for something beyond race-meetings, murders, divorce cases, and scandals in high life; that a new book, or a new development of thought, may hope to rival even these breathless interests; that the press should appeal to the higher as well as the lower instincts; and in consequence you have virtually been the founder of a great newspaper. Some time ago, you gave me the opportunity of raising an important question—to me the most important of questions—as to whether Christianity was really so obsolete to-day as its opponents glibly assume.*

We have nowadays to put up with a good deal in the way of sacrilege, but I could not stand by and see the sublime figure of Christ vulgarised to make an Adelphi holiday, and, as no more competent Eighth

Champion of Christendom appeared to be forthcoming, I ventured to play David to Mr. Buchanan's Philistine. You obligingly allowed me the use of your battlefield for the occasion. Thence sprung the following pages—though, as a matter of fact, there is not, I think, a single phrase in them reproduced from my 'Daily Chronicle' letters— and, therefore, it will hardly seem inappropriate that I should wish to associate your name with a book which owes so much to your sympathy. I have condensed in its pages much religious experience, and long and ardent thought on spiritual matters— which have ever had for me the deepest fascination. If I have said a true word for the cause of true religion, I ask nothing better. If I have missed saying it on this occasion, I shall persevere in the hope of saying it on some other.

At all events, I hope you will accept this ' Religio Scriptoris' as a token of my gratitude for your many kindnesses, and believe me

Yours sincerely,

Richard Le Gallienne.

*Mulberry Cottage, New Brentford,
26th October 1893.*

THE CONTENTS

a Literary Man

VII

ESSENTIAL CHRISTIANITY

X

POSTSCRIPT

The Religion of a Literary Man

I

PRELIMINARIES

IN spite of valiant exemplars to the contrary, we would seem to insist more and more that the writer, like the tailor, is but the ninth part of a man ; and that one of those poor literary infusoria, 'the minor poets,' should have his speculations on the greater issues of life, that he should, like the Hottentot, have his 'idea of a Supreme Being,' is matter for boundless astonishment. Many indeed would seem to find the idea hugely amusing. To what a fall in the general estimation of poetry does this point.

The 'minor poet' on religion !

TWO classes of objectors meet the layman on the threshold of a religious inquiry such as I am about to undertake : the professionals of two rival doctrines, the Churchman and the Man of Science.

Professional rivals : the Churchman and the Scientist.

Each insists that the subject is his inviolable property; and in proof one brings his Bible, and the other a hermetically sealed tube containing protoplasm. Well, I must be content to be the scorn of both. Yet I must guard myself against misconception as to my use of those terms 'Churchman' and 'Man of Science,' for, indeed, there are two very different types of each. Probably they are ultimately distinguished by this: that for one type the puzzle of the world is entirely set at rest by his Bible and his protoplasm (if it can be said to have been a puzzle at all to one who is so easily satisfied), while for the other his Bible and his protoplasm are but symbols of a mystery which they focus, but are far from explaining. In short, the world is

divided into natural spiritualists and materialists. For the materialists the concrete facts of existence are alone important, indeed they have no glimpse of any other, no conception of aught they cannot touch and handle, eat, or see through a microscope;

the spiritualists, on the contrary, are almost in danger of neglecting those concrete facts, so impressed are they by the transfiguring mysteries of which to their eyes they seem but the transitory symbols. To one the world is opaque, shut within the walls of form and colour; to the other it is mystically transparent, palpitating with occult significance.

A S I write, they are shooting rooks in an avenue outside my garden. The boys of the village are there in great force. Just now I sauntered down amongst them, and there in a little black heap at the foot of a tree was 'the bag.' I took up one of the poor dead cawers. It was still shudderingly warm. I took up another and another, and noticed that the heads of each were missing. 'Oh, that was to prevent them tasting bitter!' said my neighbour. And then I realised that the one significance of these poor dead things was 'rook-pie'! Up went the ugly gleaming tube. Bang! In an instant came the sound of a body toppling through the branches, and another young rook was on its way to rook-pie. In a twinkling one of the urchins seized hold of him, and had nonchalantly wrenched away his head and cast it in the grass within half a minute of his final caw up among the green boughs. Well, I know it is morbid sensibility. I know I ought to take a manly delight in slaying my feathered fellow-creatures. All the same, I could not get the thought out of my head that half a minute before that rook had been sailing and cawing in the evening sunlight, and that before you could say 'Caw!' it was a poor lifeless lump of feathers, with its head off. Ludicrous as it may seem, here was the mystery of life and death sickeningly bare. Here were two sharply-contrasted points of view brought one against the other. 'That makes the twentieth!' grimly smiled the man of the steel tube, already looking about for the twenty-first. Yes, which of those stormily circling above there was to be the twenty-first? Which had destiny already marked with the mark of death, the corvine Valkyrior already chosen for rook-pie? There was another mystery to my ridiculous sensibility, and, not feeling equal to awaiting its solution, I came back to my desk. Before I had taken up my pen came the bark of the gun, and I knew that the fatal choice had been made.

What has all this to do with religion? Much. For one temperament the world means terrible and beautiful mysteries—for another it simply means 'rook-pie.' For the mariner the stars, so eloquent to the lover, are but celestial signposts, set there, forsooth, to pilot his poor voyage; for the farmer the mysterious beauty of the seasons means but 'weather' and 'crops'; for the undertaker death means just—coffins.

THE world then is unmistakably and sharply divided into those who have what we may call the Spiritual Sense, and those who have it not. It is obvious that the large majority of mankind belong to the

PRELIM-
INARIES

Religion a
system of
Symbolism.

Science
also deals
with
symbols.

latter class. The churches are full of them, for, properly speaking, 'religion' as conventionally understood makes more materialists than science. Organised religion is but a form of more or less arbitrary symbolism. For some few the symbolism is alive: is, as we said, transparent, and radiant with the occult significance for which it stands. For the majority it is as opaque as the rest of their daily interests, nor, owing to their temperaments, could it ever have been otherwise. (And here we may remark, in passing, on the anomaly of a religion so essentially transcendental as that of Christianity being the authorised religion of so considerable a proportion of the earth's population. Of course, it has only become so by a materialisation common to all religions—a materialisation which makes one as valuable or as valueless as another.) Now, science as well as religion deals with symbols, for there is no single fact of life, no existence in nature, which, truly seen, is not symbolic. But how often does your average scientist realise this? In his carefully-stored observations he fondly sees explanations ; though, of course, the truer scientist only sees in them ever new centres of wonder, new revelations of the unknowable, that baffle still more than they reveal.

THE average churchman and the average scientist are, therefore, on the same plane of an unmysterious 'rook-pie,' sleep-and-eat existence ; and the only possible broad division of men from the standpoint of religion is into spiritualists and materialists. In making this distinction, of course, we must not forget that the mere necessity of existence forces us all to be in some measure materialistic. The spiritual insight is mercifully intermittent—at meal times, for example. How should we fare if cows and sheep were always to appeal to us as forms of symbolism, so that the roast lamb cried from the dish like the blood of Abel. The vegetarian is a man who is thus perpetually haunted by the symbolic nature of flesh-meat. And yet his restriction to vegetable forms is obviously illogical. If it be the brotherhood of life that the vegetarian supposes himself to be regarding, is not the cabbage also a fellow-creature, and why slay the innocent asparagus in its succulent green youth? Is it not simply that, in the case of vegetables, the vegetarian can 'murder' without a shock to his nerves, and in the case of animals he cannot? The plant may be said to die a natural, and the animal a violent, death. In one case the gore, the butcher's knife, and the pathetic pleading eye of the poor victim, do not appal the imagination. Green blood instead of red, and no moans (unless one dines off mandragora), that seems the only difference. The precious spikenard of life is spilled in each case alike, and the 'murder' is in each case unavoidable. Life, like an Eastern queen, imperiously demands death, and she must have it.

We are all, I resume, of necessity more or less materialistic, but some of us contain as well a certain leaven of spirituality, while some of us seem to contain none at all.

Whatever appeal the following naïve reflections on great matters may have to any, it will be to the person leavened with that modicum of spirituality : let us call him, for short, the spiritualist. Other persons are hereby warned against a sure sacrifice of their lives, a wilful suicide of their time.

B UT, unfortunately, 'the spiritualist' is divided among numberless small schisms ; and I must, for certain, miscarry with many, simply because I do not subscribe to that particular form of symbolism which they confuse with essential religion. The Wesleyan, the Baptist, the Anglican, the Catholic—save in that sympathetic part of him which is free of his creed—will have none of me. By another very different type I shall be no less rejected—the typical literary man of the period, who sips his absinthe (with a charmingly boyish sense of sin), and reads Huysmans. To discuss such antiquated matters

PRELIM-
INARIES

*Caveat
lector !*

Schisma-
tics.

The literary
man of the
period.

as God, Love, and Duty, when one
might be wrangling over Degas,
or grappling with a sonnet by
Mallarmé!

II

THE RELATIVE SPIRIT

BUT in spite of the survival, not
to say the flourishing existence,
of sects and schisms, we have to-day
a considerable advantage over our
fathers in approaching this question
of Religion. We are in the position
to assume gaily much that they could
only hold by dying for; though, of
course, this can only be assumed in
presence of a given audience. The
world is no more of one opinion
to-day than it ever was or is ever
likely to be. Every book is therefore dependent for readers on a certain
A Writer
but the
representa-
tive of a
tempera-
ment.
limited section of society; no writer
can be more than the representative
of a certain temperament. I said that
the appeal of these pages will in the
first instance be to 'spiritualists' (the

reader has, of course, understood that by that term I do not mean table-rappers or any other unauthorised limiters of its meaning) ; in the second place, then, it will be to those who, in Carlyle's phrase, have 'swallowed formulae'—after all, a very large class to-day ; a class which realises that, while creeds are temporal, religion is eternal. To that other class, however, which has also 'swallowed' religion itself, and looks upon the very word as obsolete, my poor words must seem but as old wives' tales.

WE are permitted to smile now at questions which were literally burning to our ancestors, such gracious heresies, for instance, as those which so 'plunged and gravelled' the soul of Sir Thomas Browne : 'that the soul might in some sort perish and rise again with the body,' 'that all men should finally be saved,' or 'that we might pray for the dead.' But these, says the gloss, 'he suffered not to grow into heresies.' Such terrible heresies as these no longer affright us. We believe them or leave them as we list, though there are few of us, I imagine, who do not, in different terms, hold the possible salvation of the whole race of man, and who do not sometimes, when the world is budding and shooting in the spring, pray softly in our own way for the souls of those beloved who are no longer with us in the sun and the sweet air.

THE most vital point at which religious controversy formerly ever arrived was the Inspiration of the Bible. But that difficulty has passed. We now either accept or reject the inspiration of a hundred Bibles, and the question is no longer of the inspiration of one book, but of the inspiration of the human soul, which has dictated all books. Once the

question was of miracles, but now we see that the authenticity of this or that isolated miracle is of little account in a world which is itself one glorious unfathomable miracle. ' Now for my life,' again to quote Sir Thomas Browne, ' it is a miracle of thirty years, which to relate were not a History, but a piece of Poetry, and would sound to common ears like a Fable.' A certain editor, commenting on this passage, remarks : 'Yet its actual incidents justify no such description'! This editor seems to me the type of man who asks for a miracle, in the ordinary sense of the word, an aberration from the usual course of Nature, a sign, a wonder, as if we had not about us far more wonders already than we have time to realise. Who that has ever been young, that has lived light in the spring, can fail to understand what Sir Thomas Browne meant by his miracle of thirty years? It was to those who cannot that Christ refused a sign. If the world with all its myriad wonders will not touch them, if through the veils of all its so transparent forms they cannot see the face of God flashing—neither will they believe though one rose from the dead. To-morrow his resurrection would be as commonplace as the telephone, and enterprising firms would be interviewing him with an eye to branch establishments in Hades.

THE RELATIVE SPIRIT

'One' (commercial) 'traveller returns.'

THE RE-
LATIVE
SPIRIT

The Trinity, the Atonement, Infant Baptism, Baptismal Regeneration, the Immortality of the Soul, the Life Hereafter—these and many other dogmas are now seen to be matters of symbolism or personal intuition.

Concerning Documents.

IT is no longer necessary for us to dispute painfully concerning documents. All such matters the German commentators and M. Renan have already settled for us, and faith has really nothing either to hope or fear from the discovery of any number of gospels. In short, we have

Blessed Divorce of Theology and Religion.

accomplished the inestimable separation of theology and religion. Our religion no longer stands or falls by the Hebrew Bible.

THERE can be no doubt that we largely owe this immense gain to science and the scientific method of study: not because science has proved or disproved this or that—for it can prove or disprove nothing that is ultimate—but because it has familiarised us with that philosophical instrument of inquiry, the Relative Spirit. By

The Relative Spirit.

its aid matters which were once regarded as final, customs and opinions
over which many a human heart has
been broken, are now seen to be
merely relative to certain conditions,
as fashions in dress, and peculiarities
in national manners are relative. Be-
coming more and more of a law unto
ourselves, we pretend less to be a law
unto others. Before the breath of that
genial spirit the icy conventions and
prejudices of mankind melt away as
frost in the sun, and the liberated
souls of men and women laugh and
are glad in the joyous developments
of their natures as God made them.

B UT—and here we approach the
centre—let us not forget, what
indeed the Relative Spirit would
itself teach us, that its jurisdiction
ends at a certain point. It carries
us too far if it causes us to imagine
that there is nothing absolute in life,
nothing which is not, after all, a matter
of opinion. Indeed its operation, like
all philosophic processes, is entirely
among forms and formulae—it cannot
dissolve the essences of things. Be-

neath every convention there is a vital principle over which it has no sway.

FOR example: it is our indolent custom here to wed but one wife. In Turkey our custom is the exception, and there it is more usual to wed four. Religion hallows, shall we say, 'the union,' morality countenances it, and it might be held that Nature itself is on its side. Now, are we to condemn that polygamous Turk as irreligious or immoral? It is probable he is both, but not necessarily because he has four wives and we only one. What we have to realise is that we may be more irreligious and immoral with our one than he with his four.

The Relative Spirit working in some might therefrom deduce that chastity of living is a mere casual condition. Morals, we have been told, are matters of geography. But that would be a superficial deduction. The question is of essential chastity of life. You may say, very properly, that it might be harder for a man to be spiritually minded with four

wives than with one, that monogamy
is a higher ideal of relationship between men and women. This one
admits ; but the question is whether,
relative to his conditions, his matri-
monial complexities, that Turk does
or does not struggle to follow the law
of his higher nature. And that is the
question which it is the business of
the Relative Spirit always to raise.
It is our guide as to what is only
of provincial and what of universal
importance in any particular custom
or law. It is the ruling of the
Supreme Courts as compared
with that of a Justice
of the Peace.

THE RE-
LATIVE
SPIRIT

III

WHAT IS SIN?

IN dealing with this Relative Spirit,
I have practically answered, so
far as I am able, one of the few
ultimate questions which that spirit
leaves us to settle. The question for
our forefathers was Pilate's question

What is
Truth?—the
question of
the Past.

WHAT IS SIN?

—What is Truth? That we may be said to have answered — relatively. We might say that truth is the best possible condition in a given set of circumstances. Relatively speaking, we have answered it; ultimately speaking, we have given it up.

What is Sin?—the question for the Present.

BUT the vital question of the modern world is *What is Sin?* So many acts our fathers have condemned are seen to be not essentially, but only relatively, evil. Their character is changing with changing conditions. Is all 'sin' thus relative, or is there such a thing as essential sin? You may remember how, in

Mr. Pater's 'Marius, the Epicurean.'

Mr. Walter Pater's beautiful psychological romance of *Marius, the Epicurean,* the young philosopher, watching the calm demeanour of Marcus Aurelius at those cruel games which the wise emperor endured because they were inevitable, shrank with horror from that cold acquiescence. Not for him so complete a triumph of the Relative Spirit as that.

'Surely,' exclaimed his soul, 'Surely evil was a real thing; and the wise man wanting in the sense of it, where not to have been, by instinctive election, on the right side was to have failed in life.' That is how Marius answered our question, a question which a man must more or less answer for himself: 'What is Sin?'

THE answer to it necessitates another question: Have I, or have I not, a lower and a higher nature? If yes, must I live in accordance with the promptings of my lower or my higher? That, as I conceive it, is the one vital question of Religion. Morality answers it for us in some measure. Man has long seen that a harmonious social existence is impossible on the lines of the lower nature. On the coarser appetites of that morality has, therefore, set a curb. Though a part answer, it is a suggestive one. The law of the higher life thus prescribed by the merely gregarious instinct of man, followed for the sake of our fellow-men, is soon seen to be lovely and pleasant in the following for its own sake; and so from a necessary condition of social intercourse flashes the intuition that such living has a higher sanction and end: That not only should we live righteously for the sake of our neighbour, but for the sake of that spark of God which we feel ever brightening within us.

WHAT then is Sin? Is it the breaking of the Mosaic Decalogue? Is it the disregarding of conventional moralities? Or is it something less, and something more?

In frankly answering this question we shall yet need for some time to come to observe certain reticences out of regard to the sensibilities of our neighbours. But we can consult such sensibilities too much, and truth is well rid of 'the weaker brethren.'

UNDER the dispensation that is quickly passing many perfectly religious exercises of natural function were condemned as evil: the desire of joy, the delight of affinities, the satisfaction of vital needs.

The Relative Spirit, however, has taught us that these *are* not sins but only *may be* under certain circumstances; indeed it will sometimes happen that what were once sins under the old *régime* become duties under the new one. Unduly 'refined,' idealistic, anæmic persons, for example, are all the better for a dip in good gross earth, a plunge in the Demiurgus cup; for the lower nature needs nutriment just as much as the higher, and it is no less misleading to treat man as all angel than it is to treat him as all beast. Certain temperaments are to be trusted with any measure of such nutriment, others with scarcely any at all. Each man must judge for himself.

Indeed the question *What is Sin?* must in every case be answered in accordance with the relations involved, and the necessities of the particular temperament: that is, by the due consideration of our duty to our neighbours, and our duty to ourselves—which are, however, both at bottom one duty.

WHAT IS SIN?

Old Sins become New Duties.

GENERALLY stated, I would define sin as that which in any time, or country, or under whatsoever conditions or outward appearances, means the living by the lower instead of the higher side of our natures. We cannot tell what that higher side ultimately signifies, any more than we can tell what that lower signifies. We only know that one is higher and one is lower—and that it is the evident intention of nature that we should live according to the higher.

I V

WHAT IS PAIN?

BUT, it may be said, I have really begged the question, eluded the problem, which is not so much of Relative Sin, as of Original Sin— in other words the immemorial problem of the meaning of evil, the

mystery of pain, the crux of theology, the darkest mystery of life.
Actually the mystery of joy no less
eludes us, but we are content to
leave that, because it squares with
our optimistic theories of the universe. We explain it relatively
by saying that God is love. But
pain, obviously, militates against such
theories, and raises the eternal question, thus expressed by Mansel and
quoted by Mr. Herbert Spencer:
'How is the existence of evil com-
patible with that of an infinitely perfect Being; for if he wills it, he is
not infinitely good; and if he wills
it not, his will is thwarted and his
sphere of action limited.'

ONE of those child's questions—
so unanswerable! As a pre-
liminary, we can only say that no
question whatever that is not relative
is answerable. Ultimate pain and
ultimate joy are alike inscrutable.
Doubtless the problem of pain arises
mainly from our limited anthropomorphic conceptions of God, the
First Cause, the Unknowable. We

WHAT IS
PAIN?

The Question stated too much in terms of our own existence.

Concerning the use throughout of the word God, see pp. 74 and 75.

inevitably figure him as a creature with like passions and senses and sentiments as ourselves. We say that we, his poor creatures, would not countenance such pain as we see about us; but in saying this we forget that we are not God, that we have but five senses and three dimensions, by which to form our judgments. We can form no possible conception of the processes of God, for the simple reason, probably, that we are a part of them. We hastily judge by two or three of the conditions within our grasp, but we might as well assume knowledge of a pattern by a coloured thread or two, or the design of the firmament from our hole-and-corner solar system.

IT is idle to put this question of pain ultimately, quite idle to ask the ultimate explanation of much simpler matters, in fact of anything in the world simple or complex. Put relatively, there is, of course, but one familiar answer, founded on observation of the working of pain here : that it is but a process, and must be judged not in itself, but by its results. Some results we are able to see, the majority we cannot see, and our only possible method is to argue from those results that are seen towards those that are unseen.

Before we arrive at any such distant point, however, the difficulties of the question may be at least reduced by a careful consideration of facts right in the foreground.

O NE has no wish glibly to explain away the real troubles of life, but it is futile to deny that they are immeasurably intensified (1) by the Sentimental Spectator, and (2) by our habit of viewing pain in the bulk. The sentimental spectator is a person of exquisite nerves. It is probable that the sufferer is not, and thus we might make a scale showing the graduated values of certain sufferings at certain points of sensitiveness. But, suppose a sorrow befalling the most highly sensitive person. Recently a friend of the

WHAT IS PAIN?

Pain a process.

The Sentimental Spectator.

writer's lost a devoted husband by a sudden and violent death. It was a very awful and heart-breaking thing. One would not have been surprised had she succumbed beneath the shock. 'No,' said an old friend of hers, 'you see, she is a woman of many interests.' It sounded a hard saying at first, but the more one reflects upon it, how valuable does it become! She was 'a woman of many interests'—how? By reason of that very sensibility of nature for which we, her friends, had feared. It was not that she did not love her husband, with that love indeed which makes the world a temple, but, as I say, the very power which made her capable of so intense an affection, made her capable of inevitable compensations as well. The loss was ten times, but the compensations were also ten times. In this way, if life does not temper the wind to the shorn lamb, it makes what wool remains the warmer.

THEN, too, we contemplate pain too much in the bulk. We speak of 'Whitechapel' as though there was not a happy person in it.

We contemplate pain much as we contemplate the rainfall in a weather-map. That inky patch represents Manchester, we say, and we pity the poor Manchester people as though all the rain fell at once, and as though every inhabitant of the town was out in it, without umbrellas. We forget in our charitable generalisation that Manchester rises every morning with at least hopes of a fine day, that it does occasionally get it, that it has patience and umbrellas for wet ones, and that its occasional fine days are all the more welcome for their scarcity. So with pain. All this dark bulk of misery is divided and sub-divided amongst countless individuals. Each takes his little bit of pain and bears it in his corner. Moving amongst all this army of darkness, though unseen by us, is another army of light, of love, of courage.

WHAT IS PAIN?

Pain contemplated too much in the bulk.

MUCH of our pity is of the same kind as that which pities a shoe-black for going bare-footed, when he, bless you, would not wear a pair of boots if you were to buy them for him. Indeed, nothing seems more certain than the relativity of pain, and the correlation of joy and pain is a commonplace. Moreover, it is especially important to remember what, in a little book on *The Mystery of Pain*, the philosophical value of which may be overlooked through its unfortunate theological

terminology, James Hinton continually insists upon: that pain borne for the love of another, the pain of self-sacrifice, is a positive joy; and that also many of our physical pleasures, such as a cold bath, involve a certain amount of pain, as, so to say, their fulcrum. To die for each other has been the immemorial *summum bonum* of lovers, to 'die for Christ' the sanctifying privilege of martyrs; and is there any example more familiar, more significant, than that of the mother, who forgetteth straight the pain that she had in

her joy that a man is born into the
world.

B UT, some one will object, in
itself pain is an evil thing.
'In itself!' It is impossible to
conceive anything 'in itself'—inde-
pendent of relations, of antecedents
and consequences. Pain has no
existence without the sufferer, and
sufferers are not all agreed upon the
matter.

It is customary to regard rheumatism as an evil, yet one has heard
pious folk thank God for their rheumatism, because it had taught them
what nothing else could—patience
and forbearance; unconsciously illus-
trating Mr. Meredith's great apo-
thegm: 'there is nothing the body
suffers that the soul may not profit
by.' Yet, you persist, rheumatism
is none the less a bad thing. How
so? Processes are to be judged
by their results. If rheumatism
is found to make me a better man,
can I say that rheumatism is a
bad thing? Rheumatism does not
exist impersonally. It exists only

WHAT IS
PAIN?

The
Sufferer
the Real
Authority.

in relation to certain, much-to-be-
pitied, individuals, and if some such
are able to say that it has helped
rather than harmed them—surely
the testimony of the brave is as
good as that of the coward. Why
should we pay heed so exclusively to the coward's statement of
life ?

The
Ministry
of Pain.

THIS is a rough illustration of
what a large proportion of
the greatest men and women in all
ages have regarded as the ministry
of pain—pain as the cleansing fire.
Such is still the courageous attitude
to-day of men so divergent in mind
as Mr. George Meredith and Mr.
Coventry Patmore. Mr. Meredith, in
his robust way, sees pain everywhere
about him as the crucible in which
life is refined, the process by which

'From flesh unto spirit man grows
Even here on the sod under sun.'

Mr. George
Meredith.

Any one who cares enough for his
salvation to thread the thorny ob-
scurities of Mr. Meredith's 'A Faith
on Trial,' will find in it the most

spiritually helpful of all recent poems. There is no modern 'thinker' profounder than he, no one who has faced more spectres of the mind. Yet he comes out of all his thinking the strongest of the apostles of faith.

MR. PATMORE even formulates a mystical luxury of pain, after the ecstatic manner of the old saints, and, personifying it, prays for

. . . the learned spirit without attaint
That does not faint,
But knows both how to have thee and to lack,
And ventures many a spell,
Unlawful but for them that love so well,
To call thee back.'

WHO has not been heartened by Browning's cold-water cure : 'When pain ends, gain ends too'; and, if the reader likes him better, here is Mr. Herbert Spencer on the subject. Speaking of, so to say, the scientific religious man as opposed to the conventionally religious, he says : 'Convinced as he is that all punishment, as we see it wrought out in the order of nature, is but a disguised beneficence, there will perhaps escape from him an angry condemnation of the belief that punishment is a Divine vengeance, and that Divine vengeance is eternal.'

BUT hereon some one produces Schopenhauer, and, as his trump-card, plays Spinoza. No philosopher so readily explains himself as Schopenhauer. His philosophy was simply the formulation of his own special disease, the expression of his own ineffably petty and uncomfortable disposition. He was a small philosopher, with a great literary gift. Spinoza, on the other hand, was a very different person: he was a great philosopher, with a comparatively small literary gift. But, says the Spinozist, according to him pain was an unmistakable evil. Joy was the vitalising, fructifying power. Let us hear Spinoza himself. Says he in his *Ethics*: 'By *pleasure* I shall therefore hereafter understand an affection whereby the mind passes to a greater perfection; and by *pain* an affection whereby it passes to a lesser perfection.' Could anything be more to the purpose of our argument? Spinoza's English commentator, Sir Frederick Pollock, seems to me confusing in his interpretation of this passage. In one case he implies that Spinoza meant actual, immediate, sensual pain—pain 'in itself'—and in another he says, 'we here use the terms good and evil as denoting the quality, not of the sensation as such (for that would only be to say that pleasure is pleasure and pain is pain), but of the events and relations in the organism immediately indicated by the sensation.'

However, there are Spinoza's own words, and if we have misinterpreted them, after all, humanity does not stand or fall by one of its great men, and we may, if we find it necessary, put Spinoza aside in favour of others even greater, who have speculated upon life no less profoundly than he.

IN this matter of pain, as in every, other under the sun, it is theory against theory, and we shall each accept that alone which suits our temperament. Each, at the same moment, is relatively true and relatively false.

HOWEVER, it is always best to put a question at its worst. Let us suppose pain as an unmitigated evil—and allowing me, for the sake of emphasis, to speak in theological terms—let us thence deduce that, whether God is all-merciful or not, He is evidently not all-powerful. Let us embrace the heresy of the Manicheans, and hold that the world is at the mercy of two rival dynasties of good and evil—God and Satan.

Well! what if the fate of man ultimately hangs on the fortune of battle, on some celestial Armageddon, why should we be afraid? Why should we so faint-heartedly conclude that God will lose the battle? He has hurled Satan out of heaven once, and shall He not hurl him forth again? And even if, impious thought, Satan should triumph, are we not men, can we not face all the pains of hell he shall devise? If he slay us outright, all is forgotten — if he keep us in torment, shall we not some day raise God's banner again?

THE truth is that our modern pessimism means but two things: cowardice and selfishness. The selfish — it is a merciful provision — always, in the long-run, suffer the most, though it may often seem otherwise. And no observing man will deny that this is, comparatively, an age of cowardice. At any rate it is an age of anæsthetics. Those who, like Mr. Henley, chant 'The Song of the Sword,' are at least so far right; and we may well pray for the spirit of our brave forefathers, who went to battle with stouter hearts than we take to the dentist.

V

FREE-WILL

BEFORE discussing two other hackneyed questions which still arise, or at least are always raised, in regard to religion, allow me to postulate : that nowhere more than in religion is it wise to do without as much as we can. One perennially discussed question is that of 'Free-will.' Is man 'a free agent,' or is he 'a machine'?—or whatever metaphor of passivity the disputant may prefer.

'FREE-WILL,' I venture to suggest, is one of those dogmas with which mankind can very well dispense. For, when one considers that will-power, like any other, is a certain fixed quantity, at most a certain fixed potentiality, within us, that evidently, therefore, wills are not equal, and that to say 'use your will' to a man who has been obviously born without one, is to misunderstand his case ; when one considers too that will is dependent on other qualities of the nature, and upon external influences, to quicken or retard it, it is hard to see that we have any more free-will than, apparently, a flower.

You say—But it is in your power to avoid this or that course. Not necessarily. At any rate, I probably want to avoid it, my will struggles to avoid it, but the other forces of my nature are too strong for my will, and they have their way. You say—Had you struggled a little more! Ah! but I could not. It is an easy sum, a calculation in simple proportion. You will resist the temptation as long as your will lasts, and when it is used up you will give in ; or if your will happens to be stronger than the temptation, you will not give in.

Is not this, one is always asked, a dangerous doctrine? Might it not paralyse effort? Does it not make men simply like clockwork? But will the clockwork stop working because you tell it that it has been wound up, and is not, as it imagines, going of itself? Besides, one does not deny that the will may be strengthened by influences from without. In those is the only hope of the weak will, but whether it shall encounter those influences depends either on accident or on the possibility of its being strong enough to seek tonics for its weakness.

Great books are among such batteries for the recharging of the will—and Emerson's 'Essay' on Self-Reliance' is, of course, a well-known preparation of phosphates.

WHEN we battle so for free-will, we forget how large a proportion of our life is outside our will, which yet we accept without a murmur. Obviously our existence, to start with, is beyond our control. Our qualities are as inexorably fixed for us as our stature. And then the friends we meet, who, as we say, change the whole course of our lives, the man or woman we marry. We are admittedly at the mercy of so-called chance in these tremendously important matters. Where is the logic of drawing the line at our own personal free-will? For how these

persons or various accidents may
affect us is not a matter for our de-
cision ; it will depend on the relative
strength of individualities and on all
the conditions. This or that new
friend influences me for good in proportion as my nature is open to good
impressions and no more ; and the
fact of our meeting—like my nature
—is an accident ; in other words, a
matter entirely outside my control.
It is simply a problem of human
chemistry.

W HAT then have we to live
for ? Is all our aspiration
and struggle a mockery ? Not at
all. Aspiration and struggle are
processes towards the development
of our nature to the limit of its ex-
pansion. Life is a reality governed
by illusions, and 'free-will' is one of
the illusions that govern it.

What have we to live for? This
question, like almost every other that
teases the mind of man, has its *raison
d'être* entirely in that primitive egotism which makes man the measure
of the Universe. The inheritor of

FREE-
WILL.

What
have we to
live for ?

The
Egotism of
Man.

an arrogant legend of his godlike origin and prerogatives, he sees about him laws in constant operation that pay no heed to his pretensions. Taught to believe that the world was made to please him, and finding it sometimes failing to do so, he grows puzzled and angry. If he could but realise that his ideas of dominion are absurd fancies, such as some African chief might cherish of his being sole imperator of the world ; if he could but take up his position as the servant instead of the lord of creation, as but one humble link in the mysterious chain of being, as but one child born to the fatherhood of God, he would smile to see how simple all his complexities would suddenly become.

When we are no longer called upon to explain Nature in accordance with the desires of one of its creatures, when we no longer stand in the centre of things, but humbly take our place in that vast circumference whose unknown centre is God, we shall see with different eyes. Then maybe we shall realise the deep meaning of the 'superstitious' old text, and count it enough explanation of the life of man to say that it exists 'to the praise and glory of God'— to the working out of His indefinable purposes ; that we are the servants of His household, the soldiers of His army, and that the pay is life! Had He willed it this glorious gift had never been ours. We might have still slept on unsentient, unorganised, in the trodden dust. But He has raised us up and endowed us with this wondrous framework of subtle vibrating being, that no tittle of the joy and beauty of His world should escape us.

M EANWHILE, however, though the astronomy of Copernicus is taught in our schools, the world still remains Ptolemaist. We still practically believe that the whole of the firmament is an immense candelabra for lighting this bit of an earth ; that it revolves round us instead of our revolving with it round some inconceivably remote centre. We are accustomed to talk as though God is

FREE-WILL

'To the praise and glory of God.'

The World still Ptolemaist in practice, though Copernican in theory.

FREE-
WILL
our servant, and that His laws must needs square with our desires. We are silly enough to talk of our rights. Man has no rights in regard to God. He has only mercies. He exists for God, and not God for him. The incorrigible presumption and irreverence

Life a
free boon.
of man! It never seems to occur to him that the joy and good things of life, which he undoubtedly possesses, have come to him all unasked and unworked for—a free boon. It is as though, invited to a great feast as a favour, we should quarrel with the host because he had not consulted us as to the *menu*, which, nevertheless, was seen to please greatly the majority of the guests. Our rights! our grievances—against God! When we have

'Counting
our
mercies.'
given due thanks for our mercies: for the mere sky and sunshine, for the wonder of love, for the miracle of beauty, for the humblest joys of sensation—then it will be time to talk about those.

IF it appears that man has actually no say in his life, that he is but clockwork, well, it is clockwork full of sweet chimes. Or let us say that man is like a flower planted here by God to grow according to His will and for some, to us, undivinable end, just as we plant daffodils in our garden plots and never tell them why. At all events, one thing is certain : that, as Sir Thomas Browne says, 'God has not made a single creature who can understand Him'; and another thing is no less sure, that it is not to the arrogant spirit of modern inquiry that He will ever be revealed.

B UT to return in conclusion to free-will, is it to be doubted that we have far more to gain by losing than keeping it ? Our precious 'individualities' are curtailed, it is true, but in the next chapter I shall venture to suggest that we exaggerate our regard for those ; and what we gain in their place is, to my thinking, considerably more important : a very precious gain in charity to our fellows, in consolation to ourselves.

We already see the humanising

Marginal notes:

FREE-WILL

The loss of 'Free-will really a gain.

influence of the more scientific view in the adoption by public opinion of such phrases as 'homicidal mania,' 'erotomania,' 'dipsomania': terms which obviously imply that man's 'sins' are not to be visited as 'crimes,' but charitably regarded as the painful operation of diseased functions, independently transmitted, and more than enough punishment in themselves.

VI

THE HEREAFTER

THE question of 'the life hereafter' is by many regarded as the most serious problem of religion. They tell us that a future life is a necessary completion of this; that in such a life alone can the injustice of this one be corrected, the forces set working in this be developed to their logical results. At the same time they postulate that future life as a state of perfection. Surely these three statements are incompatible. A life that would be the working out to their conclusion, supposing we can imagine conclusion, of the forces of this one would not be a perfect life, as we understand it, but simply a reproduction of this. Moreover, Nature does not bind herself to bring all sowings to harvest. It is one of her most familiar mysteries that she is able to waste and yet want not. No spendthrift may rival the lavishness of Nature, and the Eastern queen who drank dissolved pearl as a liqueur was economical in comparison.

FIRST let us ask : not whether the future life, the survival of personality after death, be true or not, but whether we really care about it so much as we imagine. In religion, we have said, it is especially wise to do without as much as we can. Can we then do without the idea of a future life, the immortality of the Ego, or is it a necessity of our life here ?

Let us first bring the question of personality into the foreground of our present existence, and ask ourselves if we do not exaggerate its value to us here and now.

THE
HERE
AFTER

A theory
of Friend-
ship.

FOR example, we say that we love our friends 'for themselves.' Do we mean by that that we love them, so to say, in the lump, bad and good together ; or that we love them because of their possession of certain qualities valued by us, for the sake of which, possibly, we are content to overlook certain other qualities not attractive to us, perhaps actually repellent ? Suppose we lose that friend, but shortly after meet another person who possesses like qualities. Do we feel quite the old need for the old friend, or have we not practically found him again in the new one? I do not forget the power of association, but association is a quick-growing ivy, and will shortly grow up about the new friendship as the old. And, of course, we may not make a second such acquaintance, but the chances are that we shall.

IF you answer that the new friend will probably in course of time take the place of the old one, then it is clear that it is the qualities of both, not as we say their individualities, their Egos, that we value. Actually we do not love either 'for themselves,' but for their good-nature, their wit, their beauty, or whatever their qualities may be ; and those qualities are to be met with over and over again, possibly in still more satisfying harmonies. Thus we have not to wait to meet our old friends again in heaven, we meet them again already on earth —in the new ones. Nor does such a view abolish the noble virtue of constancy ; for what generous spirit can lightly forget the men and women who have, for however short a time, been to them the vessels of the divine revelations of life. If we are constant to great qualities, we cannot be inconstant to their possessors.

O NE finds the same fallacy of personality in regard to places we live in, and indeed more or less in regard to everything with which we are for any time habitually associated. We return for our holidays to one particular place again and again, in fancy attributing to it a certain exceptional character ; yet if we are prevented

THE HERE-AFTER

The fallacy of ' Personality.'

going there and have to make trial of another place, we soon find that it was not, after all, the idiosyncrasies of our old resort, but merely the qualities it had in common with most other such places—the sky, the trees, the grass, the sea, which are good wherever we find them.

Do we love a flower 'for itself,' for its Ego, or for its charms of form or colour, which any one of its species possesses in perhaps an even greater degree?

Of course, the existence of the Ego is an obvious fact, whether we regard it as inhabiting the body or simply as including it : but what I would try to show is that we exaggerate its importance to us.

The
alleged
precious-
ness
of 'Per-
sonality.'

WE often hear people say that so precious is personality that the meanest creature living would not, if it could, change places with the highest. All I can say then is—more fool it! Such general statements are mainly fallacies, and, for my part, I can but think that, far from our individualities being so precious to

us, many of us—if we were wise—
would welcome a general return to
the melting-pot in the hope of a
better start next time.

ANOTHER favourite reflection
on this subject is : that, if there
be no hereafter, all the precious spiritual and intellectual acquirements of
our lives have been stored for nothing :
our character been laboriously built
up, our sensibilities exquisitely at-
tuned, to no end.

BUT how so? Have they not
been in full operation for a
lifetime? 'Tis a pity truly that the
old fiddle should be broken at last;
but then for how many years has it
not been discoursing most excellent
music. We naturally lament when an
old piece of china is some sure day
dashed to pieces; but then for how long
a time has its beauty been delighting
and refining those, maybe long dead,
who have looked upon it!
　If there were no possibility of more
such fiddles, more such china, their
loss would be an infinitely more

serious matter ; but on this the sad-glad old Persian admonishes us :

'. . . fear not lest Existence, closing your
Account and mine, should know the like
no more ;
The Eternal Sákí from the bowl has pour'd
Millions of Bubbles like us, and shall pour.'

Nature ruthlessly tears up her replicas age after age, but she is slow to destroy the plates. Her lovely forms are all safely housed in her memory, and beauty and goodness sleep secure in her heart, in spite of all the arrows of death.

B ESIDES, in many cases, we strangely misconceive, and overvalue, the acquirements of our existence. When a learned man dies, for example, we hear the newspapers bewail the amount of learning that has gone with him. To think of all that Latin and Greek and Hebrew, Egyptology and numismatics and conchology and what not, run to waste in the grave ! If he could only have taken it all with him ! But, then, supposing a hereafter, what possible use would he find for numismatics in heaven? So frequently we lament the leaving behind upon earth of gifts and gains which have no conceivable value elsewhere. And in regard to the loss sustained by his countrymen in the death of that learned man, is it not an axiom that such people always 'leave the world better than they found it'?

But, supposing that he has not bequeathed his learning in his own books, it either exists already in the books of other men or in the actual facts of which it could be no more than observation. And even supposing it all lost—which is impossible—is it so very great a matter? Learned men are merely catalogues to the library of the universe, and there are forces constantly engaged in compiling such catalogues.

All a man earns here he can spend here, and if he chooses to hoard it, it is his own affair, and probably no great loss to us. For no man that has anything of real ultimate value to his fellows can keep it to himself. He may withhold his learning, and bury his wealth; but his character— his love, his strength, his tenderness;

these, the only gifts worth consider-
ing, he cannot hide, and the operation
of them he is powerless to limit.

The Here-
after as
Compen-
sation.

BUT, you remind me,—what of
those unhappy people to whom
reference was made at the beginning
of our inquiry, those who have had
but a poor show in life, been unfortunate and oppressed? To consider
them is but to reopen the whole question of the mystery of pain. I can
only repeat that we are not the best
judges of other people's joy and sorrow, and that those we pity are very
likely not so badly off as they seem
from our point of view. For the most
unlucky the proportion of joy in life
is probably greater than we usually
admit, and it is surely a mistake to
measure joy and pain by duration in
time. Then, some natures are more
grateful than others. While the weak,

The Braver
View.

perhaps, always believe in a hereafter,
the brave have faith in their past.
They do not forget that they too
had once their purple hour, and find
courage to bear the subsequent pain
in the thought of it. Offer them their

lives over again and they would probably accept them.   Theirs is the
manly, grateful temper of him in Mr.
Davidson's poem, who said :

THE
HERE-
AFTER

Mr. John
Davidson'
'Fleet
Street
Eclogues.'

> I think that I am still in Nature's debt,
> Scorned, disappointed, starving, bankrupt,
> old,
> Because I loved a lady in my youth,
> And was beloved in sooth.'

BESIDES, if, in supposed justice,
we assume a future life for the
sake of those 'who fail'd under the
heat of this life's day,' it seems hard to
imagine them any better off.   Even
for any consideration it is impossible
to conceive a toy heaven, with all set
right ; and supposing that we postulate cycles of existence after the Bud-
dhist dream, would the weak in this
life be the strong in the next?

The
Hereafter
a belief for
the Happy
rather
than the
Unhappy.

Moreover, lovely as that dream is,
I fancy that its appeal is most to the
happy.   For the happy life seems so
good that they would it might go on
indefinitely through ever-ascending
circles ; for the unhappy, may be, it
seems so sad that they would give
thanks to have done with it, once

and for all. Anything short of the perfect life, or the perfect death, seems too great a risk; and you could bring them no gladder news than Mr. Swinburne's—

'That no life lives for ever,
That dead men rise up never,
That even the weariest river
Winds somewhere safe to sea.'

I HAVE not felt it necessary here to traverse the various familiar arguments for and against the immortality of the soul. They are in print for those who need them, and will be accepted or rejected in accordance with the needs of individual readers. Those who want to believe in a future life can do so. No philosopher can rob them of it, and probably the arguments are the stronger on the side of belief. Even if it be an illusion, illusion, as we have said, is one of life's methods. My wish is to insist that, whichever theory be true, it does not really much matter. We can do without the hereafter and the Sadducee need not make us afraid. The life here is sufficient to itself.

Practically we admit it, by the way in which we paint the supposed next life in the colours of this; it is only theologically that we doubt it. Our clinging to personal identity is an illusion. We do not really cherish it so much as we imagine. What we do cherish is living—and what matter if we live again in our present individuality or a new one? After the dip in Lethe, we shall not know the difference. That we shall live somewhere in some continuation of qualities and forces is certain: so much of immortality is at least assured us.

VII

ESSENTIAL CHRISTIANITY

THE reader may be aware that I have undertaken these notes to answer for myself a question raised by myself à *propos* of a poem by Mr. Robert Buchanan. Here I have nothing to do with Mr. Buchanan's poem, but only with one or two of the wild and whirling answers to that question. Mr. Buchanan's final position—or one of his final positions!—was, I think, that Christianity stood or fell by that belief in the hereafter which we have just been discussing.

IT is perfectly true that according to our English version of the New Testament Christ did make many definite assertions about the life to come. He promised it as a reward to the righteous, He brandished it as a threat to the sinner. But we must not forget that Christ confessedly taught in parables, and we are at liberty to conclude that He spoke in them oftener than He perhaps felt it desirable to admit. It is quite possible that He used the phrase 'the life eternal' as Spinoza used it, as Browning has used it in his beautiful phrase 'the moment eternal,' and it seems nearly certain that He used the term Heavenly Father in a sense very far removed from the customary anthropomorphic interpretations of its meaning. A gloss on the recently discovered gospel reads for 'My God, my God, why hast Thou forsaken me?' 'My strength, my strength,' etc., which, whatever its authenticity, is not without significance.

IN whatever sense Christ used such phrases, it is certain that His evangelists have distorted their importance out of all proportion to the rest of His teaching. Only thus has it become possible to represent Christianity, as it was recently represented, as a religion entirely devised for cloudland,

Christianity
pre-
eminently
a religion
for this
world.

> 'a dream for life too high,
> It is a bird that hath no feet for earth.'

A more unwarrantable mis-statement could not well be. There is nothing with which Christ's utterances have more to do than the life here. Conduct—to its ultra-ideal developments —is His constant theme. But, objects the critic, His very ideals of conduct are impossible, quixotic, beyond the reach of human nature. Surely an ideal is an ideal simply because it outsoars human nature. And, quixotic or not, can any critic of Christianity deny that as men are seen to approximate to its central teaching of self-subjection they are seen to be happy, and that the further they are seen to diverge from it the more wretched do they become. At least Christ put His finger on the central source of man's misery—eliminate self, and you have done all.

THE merely historical question was raised whether Christianity was in the ascendant or not at the present time. Some, taking isolated doctrines, such as the hereafter, answered in the negative ; some even seemed to think that, tested by that very central teaching of self-sacrifice, it was on the wane. Mankind was harder and more selfish than ever. But this seemed to have been generally felt to be a misconception, obviously disproved by the wide spread of philanthropic feeling, the far-reaching development of those democratic conceptions which are undeniably based on Christ's uncompromising communism, His gospel for the poor.

It was gladly admitted that the merely ecclesiastical incrustations of Christ's teaching were certainly being cast away; but for that very reason, it was urged, the veritable doctrines underlying them were exercising greater power than ever.

SOME said that those doctrines claimed to be 'essential' to Christianity were no less the property of other religions. This no man would think of denying. The significance of Christ as an historical figure is not so much that He was the prophet of any absolutely new religious intuitions, as that He gathered up into one masterful synthesis those that had enjoyed but an isolated expression aforetime. The intense spirituality of the Hebrew, the impassioned self-annihilation of the Hindoo, the joyous naturalism of the Greek: He combined all these in an undreamed of unity, and gave to it the impetus of His own masterful, emotional individuality.

It was not the other-worldliness alone of His teaching that was its

ESSEN-
TIAL
CHRIST-
IANITY

The
Humanity
as well as
Spirituality
of Christ's
teaching.

significance, but the everyday humanity that was likewise blent with it. Christ preached the life here no less than the life eternal, and He emphasised both as no other teacher has ever done. He not only gave an impulse to the immemorial intuitions of man, but He realised them with an unprecedented intensity of conviction. Self-sacrifice with Him became a passion, the apprehension of the spiritual significance of temporal life an actual vision. And He affirmed both in wonderful hyperboles, which have of necessity in the course of time suffered misunderstanding and distortion.

Truth
inevitably
soiled in
its trans-
mission
through the
hands of
Apostles
and Priests.

THERE must inevitably, said M. Renan, be something *borné* about the apostle of any creed, and the apostles of Christ have been no exceptions to the rule. How Christ's radiant intuitions have been materialised into opaque dogmas, no one need be told. The mistaken aim of Christian teachers has been the mistake of all teachers of ideal creeds, to bring down the ideal to the comprehension of the lower side of human nature—which accomplished, it is of no further use.

Organised Christianity has probably done more to retard the ideals that were its Founder's than any other agency in the world. Moral teaching without spiritual significance is of little force. The ecclesiastics into whose hands Christianity soon fell, being, as the majority of ecclesiastics must be, unspiritually minded, darkened the symbolism of Christ, and thus deprived the moral side of His teaching of a great part of its motive force.

CATHOLICISM, for example, is simply average humanity in a surplice—that is the secret of its hold upon the world. It practically admits that Christian ideals are hopelessly out of reach, though it theoretically preaches them, more rigidly, perhaps, than any other creed. Indeed, as one very well understands, the Catholic Church is a form of symbolism. It is of the

ESSEN-
TIAL
CHRIST-
IANITY
essence of a symbol that it stands for something which transcends itself. A Catholic priest, for example, is a symbol of what a man, according to one mistaken version of Christ's teaching, should be. Illogical people may point out that his life does not square with his transcendental creed.

Concerning
Priests.
But what of that? A man may not be at once the symbol and the thing symbolised, and a priest, like a policeman, is not always on duty.

CHRISTIANITY, like every other form of idealism, has suffered degradation at the hands of its exponents. Even its very earliest professors, Christ's own disciples, were long in realising that the kingdom He promised them was no earthly one, and had no bearing on Jewish-Roman poli-

The
Tragedy
of the
Idealist.
tics. It is the tragic fate of the idealist ever to be thus misunderstood, interpreted with a base literalness, by his own followers. A throng of idealists is an impossibility. Their talk is of heavenly bread, but their thoughts are of the earthly; and without the

miracle and the twelve baskets full
of fragments no teacher can hold
them beyond a day in the wilderness.
One recalls the sublime figure of
Brand, with his great dream of a
church not made with hands, as he
strides with inspired gaze in front
of his horde of earthly-minded bur-
gesses, whose so different dream is
but of a church of stone and lime,
with a tower and an organ that shall
put the neighbouring parishes in the
shade—a poor, little pathetic muni-
cipal triumph. Brand is, indeed, the
tragic type of the idealist through
the ages, and his followers the type
of his converts.

TIME would seem to love bitter
ironical jests, and surely it
had never a stranger one to amuse
it than the curious logic of cause
and effect, which, from a pure teaching of the spirit, a sweeping crusade
against dogmas and formulae, has
resulted in an intricate system of
rites and ceremonies, narrow and unspiritual as was ever enforced by
Scribe and Pharisee ; which, from a

ESSEN-
TIAL
CHRIST-
IANITY

Ibsen's
'Brand.'

The
Paradox
of Christian
History.

teaching of poverty, meekness, and simplicity, has evolved the proudest and most luxurious theocracy known to history. It is thus by insidious artifice that the world has so far conquered its turbulent, inflammatory spirits. Not by repression, but by a pretended acquiescence ; not by the persecutor but by the priest, has the world so far won the battle against Christ.

One can hardly wonder that the word Christian, which, maybe for some of us, strikes such a heavenly chime of association, should for many others be a name of veritable execration ; and, illogical as it may be, the world can hardly be blamed for looking at the example before the precept—of putting in harsh contrast the creed and the history of Christianity. It is but a rough reasoner, and when the Christian talks of loving his enemies, it bethinks it of the Inquisition and Smithfield ; when he talks of losing all for Christ, it forms a Titian-coloured picture of the Vatican ; when he talks of the happy lot of those who serve the Cross, it recalls only a bitter fanaticism which has so often trodden under foot the gentle and joyous innocencies of nature.

YET, nevertheless, the history of Christianity has very little to do with the teaching of Christ, and any deductions drawn from it against that teaching are entirely irrelevant. We have been told that the world has tried the Gospel of Christ and found it wanting. To that the answer is simple : the world has never tried the Gospel of Christ, and in this nineteenth century of the so-called Christian era, it has yet to begin.

SOON after the first purity of Christian evangelisation passed with its temporal successes, the ceremonial paganism which it had driven out from the old temples slily stole by the back way into the new ones, and thus conquered the young creed at the very moment when it seemed

to have been conquered by it. The
paganised Christianity which was
the result, the world has certainly
tried and found wanting. On the
other hand, fanatical developments
of Christ's teaching, which, in mistaken zeal for one side of it, neglected
to observe that harmony of the
whole which is so vital, have been no
less harmful to the world. Between
the ritualistic priest who practically
nullified its spirituality, and the de-
votee who ignored its humanity, the
vitalising principle entirely escaped,
save for certain fortunate spirits
and happy little communities of
saints.

The World
was not
ready for
Christ-
ianity.

BUT, indeed, the world was obviously not ready for so simple
and profound a gospel. It had yet to
pass through material preoccupations
which made it impossible even to
consider a philosophy that regarded
such interests with so mystical an eye.
It was still too occupied with Time
and Space to waste either on Eternity.
Great shadowy lands beyond the
horizon of the world still glimmered

in the imagination, with something almost of a spiritual mystery. America and Australia were still Hesperides fascinating the adventurous instinct of man. Great material forces such as steam and electricity had yet to be discovered and tamed. Most important of all, Copernicus had to be reckoned with. We perhaps hardly realise the profound spiritual significance of that heretical 'new' astronomy, which Galileo might only whisper under his breath. Anathematised as it was by the Catholic Church, it was the most truly Christian discovery ever made— for it at once rendered it possible for all men to look upon the world and the kingdoms thereof in that true perspective, which only a few had previously been able to divine by fortunate intuition.

I T may be said that our material preoccupations are far from ended, that scientific discovery is 'in its infancy'; but though that be true in a limited sense, it can never again be true as it was four hundred years ago. The brain of the world is not so

Margin notes:

ESSEN-TIAL CHRIST-IANITY

Material preoccupations.

The spiritual significance of Copernicus.

The true perspective of Life.

exclusively employed on such matters as aforetime. They are no longer so universally momentous, and, instead of covering the whole domain of thought, are now only provinces therein, presided over by specialists. In short we have, I repeat, found the true perspective of life. Man, like a settler in a new country, has all these centuries been occupied in making his home habitable, in building and planting, in cutting roads, in studying the climate and the bearings of his new home. Presently, it is to be hoped, he will need to be less busied about these things, and be able, after all his preparations for living, to sit him down and actually begin to live.

A simile of Man.

THE teaching of Christ is, as we have said, simple, but it is the simple which is always the hardest to understand : for complexity like mechanism may be puzzling, but it is never profound—patience can always unravel it ; it is a compound and can readily be reduced to its elements ; but simplicity is, as it were, an

The Complex is always obvious, it is the Simple that is mysterious.

element in itself, and is profound with
the profundity of deep clear water.
The complex may be a riddle, but the
simple is a mystery. The apprehension of Christ's profound simplicity
is the reward only of long and complex spiritual struggle—except, of
course, in the case of those happy
ones who come into it at birth
as into an inheritance. It is the
simplicity which can only come of
experience—or genius.

THE world has now passed through
much of that experience which
alone could make possible its realisation of Christ's simplicity. It has
sought happiness in wealth, in empire,
in luxury, and found them vanity; and
it is already turning wistfully towards
that simple life of the early world,
which it lived before it was led astray
by the *ignis fatuus* of 'civilisation.'
If the Christian era has exemplified
but little the Christian ideal, at least
it has by its mistakes proved the
truth of that ideal.

ESSEN-
TIAL
CHRIST-
IANITY

The World
more
ready for
Christ-
ianity.

ESSEN·
TIAL
CHRIST·
IANITY

Christ
the one
authority
on the
Christian
Ideal.

AS to what that ideal is, Christ Himself is the one authority and example. It is idle to cite the lucubrations of theologians or the unfaithful lives of those who are but Christians in name. In discussing a scientific theory we do not insist on its mistaken expounders, we go direct to its original discoverer. How is it that in discussing the Christian ideal the authority last referred to should be that of its Founder?

CHRIST'S teaching was an impassioned morality based upon a profound mysticism. Very soon that mysticism became hopelessly perverted by teachers incapable of understanding it, and the dogmas into which it hardened almost entirely obscured its morality as well.

The Church soon began to insist on the mere ingenuities of theology rather than the vital necessities of conduct. Christ's parabolic utterances became materialised into statements of literal fact, and instead of a spiritual apprehension of them, a merely intellectual realisation was

ESSEN-
TIAL
CHRIST-
IANITY

demanded. When Christ declared that He had 'seen the Father,' His earthly listeners at once pictured a visible bodily meeting: they had no inkling of that exalted mood of the spirit when the meaning of the world seems to become suddenly crystal-clear, the solid earth to grow strangely transparent, and, like a dove flying across the deep serene, comes the clear sweet voice of the soul of the world calling faith and peace to the soul of the creature.

When Christ spoke of the kingdom of heaven, they pictured it simply as a fairer earth rocking at anchor in the deeps of the blue sky: an essentially earthly kingdom with good appointments at court and un-limited gratification of earthly de-sires. The apprehension of it as a rapt state of the spirit, a state into which it has learnt to soar above the pains and preoccupations of earthly life, while still 'in the body,' was far from them. To tell such that the soul of a good man is heaven is to disappoint, and even Giles Fletcher's lovely description

Giles
Fletcher's
'Christ's
Triumph
after
Death.'

of the peace of the blest must, it is to be feared, seem tame to those who have looked for joys spiced with more of the pungent condiments of earth :

' It is no flaming lustre, made of light ;
    No sweet concent, or well-tim'd harmonie :
Ambrosia, for to feast the appetite,
    Or flowrie odour, mixt with spicerie ;
    No soft embrace, or pleasure bodily ;
And yet it is a kinde of inwarde feast,
A harmony, that sounds within the brest,
An odour, light, embrace, in which the soule
    doth rest.'

It is only Christ's moral precepts that are to be taken literally : the law of love, the duty of humility, the subjection of self, and the purification of the heart. All the rest is parable—mystic hints of the blessedness of the emancipated spirit, which are but darkened and debased by ignorant sensual interpretations. Beyond any teacher that ever lived Christ was the prophet of Love, through all its natural and mystical developments. That is His complete significance. The true Christian is the perfect lover, and those whom it helps to associate their lives with moving names may ' without usurpation assume the honourable style of a Christian,' though they cannot sign the Thirty-nine Articles, so that they love. It is strange to reflect that up till recently the name of Christian has been denied to such, and has been allowed only to those who subscribe to the mistakes rather than the verities of Christianity.

ESSEN-
TIAL
CHRIST-
IANITY

VIII

DOGMA AND SYMBOLISM

WE have of late years been so aroused to the great dangers of Dogma and Symbolism, as illustrated by the adulteration of the pure Christian ideal, that we have been inclined to throw the whole overboard as ecclesiastical lumber. There are many whom the mere use of Christian phraseology, even in the broadest application, irritates out of all sober thinking, so associated is it in their minds with a cant which they

The soul of good in Christian Dogma.

rightly feel to be the death of true religion. It is hardly to be expected of them that they should pause to ask whether these apparently lifeless dogmas and symbols do not, after all, stand for living realities, and whether some of them at least are not the very best expression we can have for such realities.

TO take the most primal of religious conceptions, the idea of a Supreme Being. The modern thinker prefers to characterise it by some cold and clumsy circumlocution, to speak of the Great Unknown and Unknowable, of the Power not ourselves that makes for Righteousness, or maybe simply of Nature : all phrases which fail to include the most essential quality of the conception they attempt to express, namely, its awful and mysterious majesty. It cannot be doubted that the one English word for that conception must ever be simply—God. No new word, however skilfully chosen, can ever equal the word God, polarised as it is by centuries of religious usage.

To use any other is deliberately
to use a weaker one—without any
difference whatever in the conception. The modern man doubtless
prefers to speak of Nature from a desire to escape anthropomorphism, but
the desire is vain. Already even those
colourless phrases I have mentioned
begin to take on a human aspect, for
so soon as a word is capitalised per-
sonification is not far away.

BUT the value of dogma and
symbolism can be more con-
vincingly illustrated in regard to conceptions less remote and therefore
more profitable. ' Each great Catholic
Dogma,' says Mr. Patmore, 'is the
key, and the only key, to some great
mystery, or series of mysteries, in
humanity.' One may prefer the
word 'Christian' for 'Catholic,' and
be disposed to qualify the exclu-
sive nature of the statement, but
any one who has had any spiritual
(or should one say psychological ?)
experience knows it to be virtually
true. Much Christian symbolism is
doubtless entirely fanciful, but the

DOGMA
AND
SYMBOL-
ISM

The Reality
of 'Conver-
sion.'

great central symbols are as ex-
actly records of fact as any proven
scientific proposition. The dogma
of Conversion, the New Birth, for
example, is no mere figure of mysticism, but a psychological fact daily
illustrated in the lives of thousands
of persons. The change is not necessarily brought about by confessedly
religious agencies, most frequently it
comes of the mysterious workings of
natural love, but by whatever chance
influence it is set in motion, the fact
of its daily occurrence is undeniable.
A man is a brute to-day, and in a
week's time, without any apparent
cause, he is seen to be undergoing a
mystical change ; a new light is in
his face, and he is in every way a
new creature. This is no invention
of Christianity, but simply a natural
process which Christianity has included in its body of spiritual doctrine.
In like manner it has embodied the
natural sacrament of motherhood in

The Mother
and Child.

the divine symbol of the Mother and
Child—though by the addition of the
arbitrary dogma of the Immaculate
Conception it has implied an indig-

nity towards the 'natural' process of
child-bearing of which the churching
of women is an unworthy expression.
What indeed is religion but a synthesis of the natural sacraments of life?

DOGMA AND SYMBOL-ISM

WHAT also is the dogma that
man cannot be 'saved' of
himself but a recognition of the
obvious fact that he did not make
himself, and the resulting dogma of
Grace but a more impressive way of
stating man's entire dependence for
his gifts and his fortunes on a power
beyond his own control?

Grace.

AGAIN, the old theological fight-
ing dogma that man is 'saved'
by faith and not by works is seen to
be a most important truth when we
reflect that good works may be done
from the worst of motives, and that,
moreover, among the faithful they
must always depend on the means at
their control.

Faith and Works.

THEN certain methods of Christianity, such for example as
prayer, are undeniably based on deep

Prayer.

needs of the human creature. That it is an intellectual delusion to think that a supernal power sits listening to the verbal cry of our often trivial petitions, that so far as hearing in the customary sense of aural communication is concerned we might as well go pray to the rocks and trees, is no criticism of the central truth of 'prayer,' which I take to be a humble and yet exalted attitude of the spirit, in which man is put *en rapport* with certain spiritual forces, just as certain states of bodily health make him more sensitive to invigorating climatic conditions, and the reverse. Man grows in prayer, as a plant grows in its blind yearnings towards the sun.

THERE are many for whom the verbal visible act of prayer is unnecessary, natures, so to say, which can fly without wings. They are so possessed by the spirit of prayer, that all day long their eyes are meeting with objects which awaken it, sending their worshipping aspirations soaring aloft, like white birds flying towards a beautiful light. A fair

'Natural' Prayer.

face, a liberating prospect, some perfect wonder of art; these and a thousand other chance encounters of beauty, are enough to put them, metaphorically, on their knees. Others, probably still the majority, cannot attain that pinnacle of aspiration save by the scaffolding of words and outward forms, yet so long as they have attained it, what matter how they did so? The spirit of prayer like that of imagination is awakened in different persons by different objects. Some need such traditional symbols as the Madonna and the Crucifix to inspire it, others again find such symbols, from the very fact of their long familiarising usage, void of appeal. Their virtue has gone out of them. Unfortunately it is in the nature of symbols either to wear out, or to become mere idols. A change of symbols is one of those needs of humanity that the Christian Church has not recognised.

AND here we come to the central mistake which has lessened the power even of such of her symbols as are of actual truth and universal application : the mistake of fencing off certain symbols within a sacred enclosure, and saying ‘ these only are holy,’ instead of recognising that everything moved by the breath of life is sacred and symbolic. In this respect such a book as Whitman's *Leaves of Grass* is more helpful than *The New Testament*—for it includes more.

With our growing sensitiveness to the wonder of life, we are aware that there are great and beautiful presences in it to which in Christian dogma we find no reference, and for the embodiment of which we have to turn say to the Greek mythology,

Pan and
Christ have
both a place
in the
human
Pantheon.

and to such figures as Pan, Aphrodite, and Apollo. Neither are these gods dead, nor is there actually any strife between them and the sadder figure of the Galilean. All the gods of all the creeds supplement or corroborate each other. One nation has been gifted with intuitions of certain sacred aspects of life, another with others. The Greek's joy in natural life is a good thing, but the Galilean's message of its subordination to the spiritual life was no less a necessary truth. Enabled as we are by our modern historic sense to gaze back over the whole course of the river of time, we should be able calmly to realise that every age has made its contribution to the fabric of religion : that no so-called dream which has drawn upward the mind of man has been without its spring in some appealing need of his spirit, no strange flower of 'delusion' but has borne within it the seed of some exalting ideal.

IT is perhaps idle to speak of the future, for the future no more than the present can present a uniformity of religious doctrine. The old systems will, of course, continue side by side with the new ones, so long as temperaments survive that are in need of them. By the 'future' one rather means the tendencies of the more actively religious of mankind. Such have long since felt the need of a more universal symbolism, one less based on provincial historical associations than much of the sym-

DOGMA AND SYMBOL-ISM

The Religion of the Future.

bolism of Christianity. Many such, of course, have gone out already from the old church : some for the reason that their intellectual faculties are more alert than their spiritual— with the result that not only do they deny the efficacy of church symbolism, but deny also the spiritual facts which for others remain after intellectual criticism has done its worst. These latter, again, finding their spiritual intuitions hampered rather than helped by organised systems of dogma and rite, will probably continue more and more to find their symbols in the aspects of nature and the creations of art ; 'content,' like Mr. Norman Gale,

'to know that God is great,
And Lord of fish and fowl, of air and sea—
Some little points are misty. Let them wait.'

The recent popular developments of the study of music, painting, and literature are undoubtedly due in great measure to the homeless religious spirit having taken refuge in those and kindred arts—with Browning and Ruskin societies, Ibsen theatres, Wagner revivals, and Burne Jones exhibitions for its sometimes

grotesque manifestations. The great
dogmas of the religion of the future
will be Love, Beauty, Purity, and
Strength—and the artist
will be its priest.

IX

THE RELIGIOUS SENSES

TO speak of natural religious
senses will seem redundant to
any one familiarised with the obvious
idea that everything that exists, religion included, is 'natural,' that :

'. . . Nature is made better by no mean,
But Nature makes that mean : over that
art
Which you say adds to Nature, is an art
That Nature makes.'

But one has been so brought up to
regard religion as something super-
imposed upon our human nature,
rather than something blossoming
out of it, that the habit clings. Religion, we are accustomed to think,
is an accomplishment taught in

schools, like algebra, an 'optional'
subject indeed, and we may, if we
will, learn drawing instead. To think
of religion as a natural function like
seeing, eating, or sleeping, would
seem to perplex many people, who,
indeed, would be at a loss how to be
religious without church and prayer-
book. To abolish all the churches
and to make a bonfire of prayer-
books would be a sure way to discover
the truly religious.

I HAVE already spoken of the
Spiritual Sense. By it I mean
an attribute of mind which qualifies
certain people to apprehend what we
call spiritual matters better than other
people without that attribute. And
one can illustrate it by any of the
other senses—the Sense of Beauty,
for instance. We generally admit
that certain people have a sense of
beauty, while others have not, or have
it in but an elementary degree. We
behold one man standing before a
Whistler, with face irradiated as in
the presence of the beatific vision.
To his neighbour it is as though he

saw a spirit ; and, indeed, what the one man sees is as invisible to the other as though it were a spirit. 'Do you see nothing there?' exclaims the Whistlerian. 'Nothing at all,' answers the Philistine, over-confident, 'yet all that is I see.' But there the Philistine is wrong. He evidently does not see all that is. He is not artistically clairvoyant. And so in the case of the person gifted with the Spiritual Sense. He has strong intuitions of the love of God and the sanctity and blessedness of existence. The unspiritual person has not these visions. Instead of learning from the other, he denies them : yet his denial is none the less ignorance, limitation of understanding. In matters of this kind no number of negatives are equal to one affirmative.

THE Spiritual Sense, the primary of all the religious senses, the gift, so to say, of spiritual clairvoyance, of looking beyond matter to the mysteries for which it seems to stand, may belong, indeed most frequently belongs, to what we call simple people : people quite without so-called 'culture' and 'refinement,' and 'the finer feelings.' It is not seldom found, in ludicrous forms maybe, in small country chapels, and the sympathetic may find it constantly among members of the Salvation Army. I know a 'Captain,' an out-door porter, earning less than a pound a week, at my country station, who has more spirituality in his little finger than many a Church dignitary in his whole body. To watch his face when he is talking of his conversion, quite apart from what he may be saying (which, indeed, only differs from your own feelings in its terminology), is a Church Festival, an Apocalypse, an apparition of the Divine in this dusty, work-a-day world. I have met one of his railway directors, but he was not half so interesting.

Shepherds, out-of-door 'natural persons,' as Whitman calls them, lighthouse men, men living close to the elements, most lonely men, are at bottom intensely religious. The club man may, as a rule, be taken as their antithesis. It is not the clever, but the simple, who inherit the mysteries. 'Woe is me! Woe is me!' exclaimed an old Schoolman, 'the simple brethren are entering heaven, and the learned ones are debating if there be one.'

But in addition to this spiritual sense—the religious sense, *par excellence*—there are other senses which in various ways, and to various degrees, may be described as tributaries of it: such as the Sense of Wonder, the Sense of Beauty, the Sense of Pity, the Sense of Humour, the Sense of Gratitude.

THE Sense of Wonder is obviously nearest to that spirit of worship which is the first instinct of religion, and Science is here seen to have been one of the truest friends of religion, for her discoveries must have quickened the sense of wonder in many whom the everyday marvels of life leave unmoved. The majority of mankind cannot conceive the accustomed as wonderful, and the sense of wonder is really least in that gaping populace which, at first sight, may seem to have most of it. They

THE RELIGIOUS SENSES

The Sense of Wonder.

are incapable of realising the wonder
of laws, and are only moved by that
of aberrations. It needs a comet to
arouse their sense of astronomical
mysteries. The loveliest fixed star
shines for them in vain, merely because it is 'fixed' and they have
seen it before. Monstrosities, 'novel-
ties,' 'accidents,' 'miracles,' are their
stimulants. In an average six-foot
man they see nothing to marvel at,
but a 'Chinese giant' of eight feet
they will pay much to see. Hence
Madame Tussaud's and the Catholic
Church. It is to be feared that
Madame Tussaud's stimulates but
little the sense of the higher mysteries
of existence ; yet, at the same time,
wherever we have the sense of wonder,
in however gross a form, we have one
of the germs of that spiritual insight
which sees the world and the most
'everyday' fact in it bathed in that
strange light which for some is never
gone from sea or land. Any one with
the sense of wonder must be to some
extent religious, must be emancipated in some measure from the dull
materialism of his fellows.

THE Sense of Beauty, however, is not necessarily a religious sense—save in so far as it gives birth to the sense of wonder, of love, of gratitude. Curiously enough, in our own day, among what we call *décadent* artists, we find its influence not, as one would have expected, as a spiritualising, but as a materialising, an actually degrading, influence. Even when, as I make bold to say of its worst forms, *décadent* art is not merely the expression of moral mental and spiritual disease, lusts that dare no other operation finding vent in pictorial and literary symbolism, even when it retains a certain innocence and health, it does its best to limit its appeal to what we call the sensual faculties. It merely addresses the sensual eye and ear the more obviously, and endeavours desperately to limit beauty to form and colour, scornfully ignoring the higher sensibilities of heart and spirit. The ideal of the *décadent* artist is the *cuisine*. The appreciation he expects is no different in kind, and little in degree, from that we give to a choice dish or a new

THE RELIGIOUS SENSES

The Sense of Beauty.

Its degradation in 'Décadent' Art.

liqueur. The spirit, the heart, the intellect cannot be said to take part in the appreciation of the most exquisite cookery ; and similarly there is nothing for the spirit, the heart, or the intellect in the specially ' modern' *décadent* art.

' Décadence ' mainly a disregard of proportion.

THIS *décadence* is simply the result of that modern disregard of proportion of which I shall have to speak again. It would almost seem that the relative spirit has carried us so far that we have come to deny not only ultimates, but relations also. *Décadence* is founded on a natural impossibility to start with. It attempts the delineation of certain things and aspects *in vacuo*, isolated from all their relations to other things and their dependence on the great laws of life. Its position is as absurd as that of an artist who should say: I will paint this figure in but two dimensions, and will give it no length ; or one who would say: I will paint this summer landscape, but omit all reference to sunlight. So hardly less vainly does the *décadent* attempt to ignore certain conditions of his theme, which, actually, it is impossible to ignore. To take that unsavoury example of the prismatic hues of corruption, taught us by Baudelaire. . It is perfectly true, of course, that a decaying body manifests certain beauties of colour, but to enjoy them to the full one needs first of all to suspend one's sense of smell—to hold one's nose, in short. So it is with many products of modern art. To enjoy them with any pleasure you have, in one way or another, *to hold your nose.* They may appeal to one sense of beauty, but they offend others ; for surely it is a mistake to assume that the sense of beauty is one, a mere sensibility of eye and ear. May not smell even be, so to say, an olfactory sense of beauty ! What many speak of as a sense of beauty is merely a sense of colour and form, and it were well enough if the impressions of objects were confined to colour and form—but, need one say, they are not, but go much deeper. Moral beauty and spiritual beauty are not mere

THE RELIGIOUS SENSES

Limited Definitions of the Sense of Beauty.

Beauty more than Form and Colour.

metaphors ; and a picture or a book which, whatever its appeal to our sense of form and colour, violates the sanctities of life or ignores any of its conditions, is not, properly speaking, a thing of beauty, a work of art.

NOT, of course, that I mean for a moment that art must be definitely moral or didactic. It has nothing to do with morals—only, so to say, with spirituals. Many people seem to confuse the moral and the spiritual. As a matter of fact the spiritual must often of necessity be the immoral. A man's subject may be as so-called 'immoral' as he pleases so that he is able to treat it spiritually, or shall we say symbolically, in its relation to the whole of life.

But supposing beauty to be, as certain modern artists say, merely a matter of form and colour, is it not logical that the artist should confine himself for his themes to objects which have, or at least suggest, nothing but form or colour—if such are to be found ? One is ready to admit that the whole mystery of life, 'the pathos of eternity,' is to be found in a curve. Colour in itself is a mystery, and are there not trance-like moments when suddenly we ask ourselves, why a *coloured* world, why a *blue* sky, and *green* grass, why not *vice-versa*, or why any colour at all ?

BUT the difficulty is that when an artist paints men and women, he paints objects which imply more than form and colour, implications that it is impossible to escape or elude. The artist may answer that he is able to elude them. To him, as it appears his mother is to Mr. Whistler, a man is simply an arrangement of form and colour. He is able to paint pain without pity and foulness without repulsion. Yet though he be able to achieve this detachment from humanity, this absorption in paint, his brush will have proved itself more sensitive, and have thwarted the artist's narrowness of intention. In spite of himself he will have painted a man, though he may persist in calling his picture an arrangement. In the empire of life, art is but a province, and, like the artist, is subject to greater laws than its own.

Men and Women imply more than Form and Colour.

Art subject to greater laws than its own.

WE may conclude, then, that the sense of beauty is not necessarily a religious force, but that in so far as it tends to materialism and inhumanity it may be a potent anti-religious one. It is from a perception of these dangers that religious teachers have so often been antagonistic to art.

On the other hand, that it may be a religious force of no less power, in so far as it impresses us with a sense of the sacred significance of life, is equally plain.

The Sense
of Pity
often
deadened
by the
Sense of
Beauty.

ANOTHER religious sense which, we have just hinted, the sense of beauty does not seem to stimulate, is the sense of pity, bound up as it is with the conception of self-sacrifice. The person whose sense of beauty is extremely developed is apt to be somewhat cruel in his attitude towards those who do not arouse his favourite sense. To be plain, with him, is to be despised; 'to be fat' literally, as with Falstaff, 'to be hated.' He cares for nothing but fair and distinguished persons and things. He has little or no appreciation of character or virtue.   In short, he is selfish, and in a great measure inhuman, as it is the tendency of all purely sensuous pleasures to make men.   Yet the sense of pity remains the divinest of all human gifts, and he who has it not indeed provokes it.   It is by pity that the strong give of their strength to the weak, the happy to some extent bring compensation to the wretched : pity is nature's correlative for pain, the gentle equaliser of life's cruel inequalities.

I HAVE heard it asked by cynical young men, who imagine that religion is at an end because they have none themselves : But why should I live for others?   Where is this law of love in nature?   Where, one might ask, is it not?   Nor could a question more completely illustrate the anarchy of thought which is at the bottom of many of our 'present discontents.' The conception of self-sacrifice is, of course, no invention of Christ, or any one teacher : it is the inevitable outcome of social existence.   It commenced long ago when barbaric man

THE RE-
LIGIOUS
SENSES

Why should
I live for
others?

THE RE-
LIGIOUS
SENSES

Unselfish-
ness an
inherent
condition of
Society.

The birth
of an Ideal.

first realised that, if he and his fellows were to live together in any comfort, it could only be on some basis of give and take. To live absolutely each man for himself could not be possible if all were to live together. In course of time, in addition to the utility, certain more sensitive individuals began to see a charm, a beauty, in this consideration for others. Gradually a sort of sanctity attached to it, and Nature had once more illustrated her mysterious method of evolving from rough and even savage necessities her lovely shapes and her tender dreams. To assert, then, with some recent critics of Christianity, that that law of brotherly love which is its central teaching is impracticable of application to the needs of society, is simply to deny the very first law by which society exists.

Self-sacrifice is no ideal dream of a gentle soul, it is seen to be a condition of man's happiness evolved by Nature for herself out of the depths of her own rough heart; and if from the stern strife of conflicting needs so fair a flower has come, how true seems the intuition of the mystic that God Himself may, after all, be Love.

I HAVE spoken of another sense not usually associated with religion. The sense of humour has often indeed seemed an anti-religious force. It has ridiculed the eccentricities of the pious, the insincerities of the devout, the soul of evil in things good. It has all along been the candid friend of religion. Therein, of course, it has done real service. In our own day we have seen it, in the hands of certain witty paradoxers, do more to hasten the disintegration of narrow religious conventions than all the German commentators together. But it is now time for these gentlemen to stop. They seem in danger of going too far, of confusing the true and false together. Recent humour begins almost to imply that goodness in itself is ridiculous, and it would seem really to believe its own witticism that 'a colour-sense is more important than the Fear of God.' In fact, our humour, like our art, has, for the present, lost its humanity. And what is humour if not the staunchest of humanists? Yet the ' new humorist ' is the bitterest, most uncomfortable, creature that crawls the planet. Kindness is surely the soul of humour ; but for it we have substituted a biting cynicism, cruel as the east wind. Our humour is indeed anæmic with over refinement. It cringes too daintily from ' the Philistine ' and ' the bourgeois ' ever to be good fun. We might indeed define ' the New Humour ' as ' the Ill-natured Remarks of the Superior Person.'

MOREOVER, it is in equal danger on another hand. Like art, it is failing to observe that proportion which is indeed its vital principle. It laughs, or rather sneers, at everything indiscriminately, and when humour does that it is near its end. It observes no reticences, respects no sensibilities, reveres no sanctities. In the two words, Ill-nature and Sacrilege, we have it all. It is mainly responsible for that lack of reverence which is one of the most depressing features of the time. Till it recognises its proper place in the scheme of existence, remembers once again that there are holy things in life which it must not approach, beautiful things it must not degrade, sad things for which it once had tears—it is no longer a friend, but one of the worst enemies of man.

THE sense of humour of which I was thinking as an ally of religion was more on the old pattern. I was thinking especially of that very essential gift which it seems to have lost awhile, the perception of disproportion. Granted this gift, there seems to me no action of the mind fitter to induce in man that attitude of humility which is one of the first principles of religion. It exults in the constant appreciation of contrasts, often invisible to other eyes. It sees human life vain and swaggering, boasting itself of its glory and power like a Nebuchadnezzar, and it turns its eyes upon the fixed stars, which have seen so many Nebuchadnezzars, and it

Marginal notes:
THE RELIGIOUS SENSES.

The proper Limits of Humour.

Humour the parent of Humility

The Tears of Humour.

THE RE-
LIGIOUS
SENSES

The
Selfishness,
Misery, and
Tragedy of
Life largely
due to a
Lack of
Humour.

smiles, but a tear steals into its smile.

THERE is no power in man more fitted to produce social harmony, to slay the devil of self, than the sense of humour. What makes a great part of the misery of life but our pretence of caring for certain baubles more than we really do, or at least should, given a sense of humour? Most tragedies arise entirely from a lack of humour. When we are jealous and passionate, the sense of humour would teach us to stop and consider. When we elbow and hustle, the sense of humour—as well as the sense of charity—would teach us to give way. Is your heart set on this particular coral and bells?—You would say to those who would surpass you in some petty way, who would sit in a better place than you, or otherwise wear feathers in the cap. Well, evidently your necessity is greater than mine ; take it ! And, instead of tearing each other, you both part happy, he happy with it, you still happier without it. Humour, then, is a religious force in that it discounts fictitious values, and minimises the petty rivalries of existence.[1]

BUT more than any other sense at all, we need one which Epictetus was constantly preaching as the great need of man, ever so long ago ; simply 'a grateful disposition,' the sense of gratitude. There

---

[1] After writing these remarks on humour as a religious force I was pleased to find the following confirmatory passage in some beautiful meditations by the Archbishop of Canterbury, entitled *Communings of a Day* :—' But to deliver sympathy from taint of sickliness, to relieve strong self-discipline of outward harshness, to give character effectiveness, to show the true naturalness of the supernatural element in Christian character, we do need that quality which has been well described as " often touching us into vitality, when sweetness alone would cloy or sicken ; which helps us to see ourselves as we are, and others as they desire to be ; whose springs lie close to those of deepest pathos ; which enters into the very essence of wisdom, gives salt to love, and makes it strong instead of sickly." In one word, we want in all our life the touch of Humour. Character—self-discipline—sympathy, all must have this salt of Humour, or they will lose their savour. And "as life goes on, we shall feel that it holds, in the economy of the human spirit, a higher, brighter, place than at first we at all recognised." '

The Religion of

is little need to dilate upon that. Perhaps nothing is so characteristic of man as his lack of gratitude. It shows deep in him from the beginning of his existence, and we can but hope that it is no more characteristic of our own time than of any other. Man forgot to say grace for his 'creation, his preservation, and all the blessings of this life,' at the beginning, and he has gone on forgetting ever since, charmingly taking all his good things for granted,—not a word about them, —but, should his little finger ache, filling the welkin with his resounding clamour against the gods.

X

POSTSCRIPT

THE reader of George Borrow will remember that amusing scene where 'Lavengro' pays a visit to a fashionable cock-pit, and is introduced to the illustrious high-priest of dog-fighting. The world, said the important doggy little man, was soon to leave everything else and take to dog-fighting. Lavengro, with the 'greenness' of a greater and simpler mind, ventured in his innocence to doubt it. Why, retorted the little great man, what was there in life a man would not give up for dog-fighting? Naïvely answered Lavengro,—'There's religion.' How one blushes for the innocent country-bred youth, with his pathetic ignorance of 'life,' so provincial, so unfashionable. Yet, oddly enough, he was right. Dog-fighting is no more, and religion still makes shift to survive.

B UT in other guises, that dog-fighter is still with us. His latest evangel has been that of the demi-monde and the music-hall. Soon, he has prophesied, 'domesticity,' with all its irksome restraints, shall be no more. Repent, for a Walpurgis night is at hand when men and women shall once more run on all fours as dogs, and revel in the offal of the streets. O happy era of liberty, when

POST-SCRIPT

The Evangel of the Demi-monde and the Music-hall.

the talon is free of the sheath for ever, and lust may run without his muzzle ; when every one may be as indecent as his heart wishes, and he who loves the gutter may lie therein without reproach ; when no man takes off the hat to a woman or a church, but all may wear it jauntily on one side, through the length and breadth of the land, may smoke and drink unmoved before the sacred passion-play of life, and expectorate with a fine carelessness, none daring to make them afraid! Such is the dream of the poor little sensual 'dog-fighter' of our days. Instead of dogs he sells us beastly and silly novels, poetry he dare not expose for sale at Farringdon market, and pathetic 'advanced' science which runs thus : 'It is a sad mission to cut through and destroy with the scissors of analysis the deli-cate and iridescent veils with which our proud mediocrity clothes itself. Very terrible is the religion of truth. The physiologist is not afraid to re-duce love to a play of stamens and pistils, and thought to a molecular movement. Even genius, the one human power before which we may bow the knee without shame, has been classed by not a few alienists as on the confines of criminality, one of the teratologic forms of the human mind, a variety of insanity.' But shall we despair of man's soul because, forsooth! a Lombroso cannot find it, of love because Paul Verlaine is a satyr, of religion and law because a mad poet fires his little pistol at Westminster. I think not. What are all these men but dirty children building their mud-pies, and soon oblivion, like an indignant mother, shall send them all to bed.

The spring of a new era is in the air—an era of faith. That prophesied Walpurgis night is already behind us ; and except in the imagination of a handful of ill-conditioned writers, artists, and 'thinkers,' who have written and painted and 'thought,' for each other, it never had even any potential existence.

'MODERN doubt' is very largely a newspaper scare, with disappointed journalists for its paid agitators, and were a census taken of the happy people in this so-called age of despair, the number would I fear be shamefully large. One has only to go to the seaside in the summer to see how full the world is of unreflecting gaiety. It contains, it is true, a small percentage of shrill-voiced pessimists, but it is far more made up of excited golfers, joyous bathers, newly-married couples, merry children, brave and patient workers, busy enthusiasts, and happy dreamers.

It is, doubtless, our duty to be unhappy, as it is the duty of the British workman to be discontented ; but when did man ever do his duty? Our very pessimists themselves in course of time marry and beget charming children, and for such desperate men make singularly gladsome husbands and fathers. The world is right not to heed its Cassandras. Whatever its sorrows and its fears, it has solid joys within reach of which it knows the virtue, and of which no weeping philosopher will ever be able to rob it.

YET, in so far as modern doubt and discontent do actually exist, the secret of them is, to my mind, entirely in man's intellectual pride. The showy results of modern science have flattered us into the idea that, after all, man can by searching find out God, that the riddle of the universe is one which his mind is capable of solving—whereas it is a riddle that can only be solved by giving it up. To 'think' less and feel more is the one cure for 'modern doubt.'

FOR has science actually brought us one step nearer to the primal mystery of things? It has catalogued the minutiae of phenomena, it has numbered the stars, it has counted the grains of sand, —but has it told us a single truth about the essence of these things, the mysterious breath of life which alone gives them significance? It has indeed quickened and deepened our sense of that mystery, but to say that every new fact has made that mystery more mysterious than ever is hardly the same as to say that it has brought us nearer to an explanation.

Science can tell us that oxygen and hydrogen will unite under certain conditions to produce water, but it cannot tell us why they do so: the mystery of their affinity is as dark as ever. It can tell us that a seed cast into the earth has certain germinating properties, by which it attracts to itself the nutriment in the soil it chances to need, and so on and so on, but what is that but a more elaborate way of stating the undoubted fact that it *grows*. It explains nothing of the miracle of the flower, nothing of the strange influence of its beauty on certain beholders. All the diagrams in the world cannot make one a penny wiser concerning the sacred mystery of motherhood. Yet the midwife and the botanist and the chemist all think they know.

The
Biologist or
the Poet?

WHICH comes nearest to the truth about love—poor Lombroso's talk about pistil and stamen, or one of Shakespeare's sonnets? There is a certain type of man who always thinks it an explanation to point to the root, as if the root was ever any explanation of the flower—and as if roots themselves had not deeper roots, and those roots had not roots again deep in unfathomable eternity. If the fine flower of spiritual love has its roots in coarse and quaint physical facts, is it not thus rather the more than the less a mystery? 'Is it not strange,' asked Benedick, as Balthasar twanged his guitar, 'that sheep's guts should hale souls out of men's bodies?' Strange indeed, but it is only the fool that thinks 'sheep's guts' an explanation. This same type always thinks he has explained a phenomenon when he has called it 'physical,'—as if the body were any less a mystery than the soul,—which reminds one of Blake's profound saying that, 'even our digestion is governed by angels.'

PROCESSES are no explanation of results. There is a point where all the operating causes seen working towards the given end are suddenly lost sight of in the flash of creation. 'Out of three sounds' the

POST-
SCRIPT

musician frames 'not a fourth sound, but a star.' It is likewise with the writer and the painter. The critics of both may analyse the subtle and complex harmonies of words and colours up to the very moment preceding creation, but the rapid synthesis, 'the miracle,' which makes of common dictionary words a line of Keats, of pigments of earth and oil a 'Gioconda' to haunt the world for ever, escapes them. How much more so is it, then, with the master-artist Nature? That flower which Tennyson took from the crannied wall, and threw down as a challenge to men of science, still lies unattempted. All the sciences together cannot tell us properly what it 'is,' and certainly all the sciences together cannot tell us 'what God and man is.' They tell us many small details 'about it and about,' but of the one thing we long most to hear, 'the miracle,' they never have told, and probably never can tell, a syllable. It is to the saint, the mystic, and the poet, that we must look for such knowledge.

Where
Science
ends Reli-
gion and
Poetry
begin.

ANTHROPOLOGISTS have recently been attacking religion by methods similar to those employed by biologists against love. By an elaborate chain of deduction which would make a theologian blush, they have decided completely to their own satisfaction that ancestor-worship and such rude beginnings of religion explain all. Here again we have the 'root' fallacy. To say that the first gropings of the religious instinct in man took these rude forms does not explain away the religious instinct. To say that a spark leaps from the impact of two flints does not explain the mystery of fire. It is Nature's way to produce her results by apparently the most irrelevant and wrong-headed means. Supposing that the anthropologists are right, what does it matter? To show that religion as we now understand it began as something very different, is no more argument against the reality of religion than the fact that the flower began as a root, the cousin of dirt and worms, would be an argument against the reality of the flower. However the religious instinct has evolved,

The
Anthropo-
logist's
'explana-
tion' of
Religion.

it is now a fact in the constitution of man, a fact as assured as the organs of digestion, and to ignore it is to be not so much irreligious as unscientific.

' LA religion,' wrote Renan in one of his noblest outbursts, ' n'est pas une erreur populaire ; c'est une grande vérité d'instinct, entrevue par le peuple, exprimée par le peuple. Tous les symboles qui servent à donner une forme au sentiment religieux sont incomplets, et leur sort est d'être rejetés les uns après les autres. Mais rien n'est plus faux que le rêve de certaines personnes qui, cherchant à concevoir l'humanité parfaite, la conçoivent sans religion. C'est l'inverse qu'il faut dire. . . . Supposons une humanité dix fois plus forte que la nôtre ; cette humanité-là serait infiniment plus religieuse.'

It is a strange thing that the very men whose one dogma is ' evolution ' should so persistently ignore the most significant illustration of their own great law. If man were once an ape, there is all the more likelihood that he will some day be an angel.

NO one less than the man of science should need to be reminded that nothing comes into existence without an impelling need. If the religious instinct had not thus arisen, it would have died of atrophy long ago, and so soon as it can be proved a useless attribute man will not be long in growing out of it. The question is : Are there not impressions borne in upon the soul of man as he stands a spectator of the universe which religion alone attempts to formulate? Certain impressions are expressed by the sciences and the arts. 'How wonderful!' exclaims man—and that is the dawn of science; 'How beautiful!'—and that is the dawn of art. But there is a still higher, a more solemn, impression borne in upon him, and, falling upon his knees, he cries, 'How holy!' That is the dawn of religion. The all-pervading sanctity of life—that is the one message which, howsoever encumbered by formulae and perverted by superstition, religion has had to deliver. Maybe all those formulae and superstitions have been

POST-SCRIPT

The *raison d'être* of the Religious Instinct.

The Sanctity of Life.

the necessary husks to protect the precious seed across the ages ; but, whether or no, the grateful, reverent spirit will always remember, in dealing with such, that it is from the ark of the old church that the dove of the Holy Spirit has flown.

SOON maybe we shall need no churches and no service-books ; not in Jerusalem, nor in this mountain, shall we worship the Father, but unceremoniously in spirit and in truth. ' The kingdom of the Father

has passed,' said an old mystic, 'the kingdom of the Son is passing, the kingdom of the Spirit is to come.' As we look around us and see side by side a growing disregard of the old externals of religion, with an increasingly passionate care for its informing essence, may we not hope that the era of the Spirit is at hand ?

RELIGION is the most ancient of the sciences. Like every other science it has made its mistakes, but essentially it has been— what cannot, perhaps, be said of any

other science—right from the beginning. Man has not waited to be
saved by biology any more than he
waited to be saved by Christianity.
There has always been more than
enough truth in the atmosphere for
the needs of the race. We are a
wondrously wise century, and with
the presumptuous certitude of youth
we decry the centuries that have
given us suck. Yet what have we
added to the sum of the world's
treasure compared with the ages
lying asleep in their graves? The
very ideas over which we wax most
proud are merely applications of wisdom which the past has been preaching for hundreds of years. What is
our boasted evolution but a corrobora-
tion of the intuitions of ancient Hindoo sages and poets? and where has
our crowning dogma of democracy
come from if not from the republics
of Greece? Our art confessedly is
imported from the past, and we cannot even design a chair or build a
house without going a century back
for advice. And our books—do we
read our own? or have not our

Our vast debt to the Past.

Our most distinctively 'modern' Ideas.

Evolution.

Democracy.

Art.

Literature.

libraries been written for us, from ceiling to floor, by the dead? We turn our faces to the future as if there lay our treasure, and the past, like an old and faithful friend, stands unheeded at our side. But the wise and the grateful soul is not so. He lives in the constant thought that all he is the past has made him, and he is very tender to 'the old perfections of the earth'—to borrow a beautiful phrase of Lord De Tabley's.

And of religion this is truest of all. The great prophets and saints belong to the past. Their message is sometimes swaddled in antiquated verbiage, but we do not cast away our old poets for that reason, and with one as the other we have only to translate them into the language of our own time to find their message true to-day as of old. As a modern painter must learn from the old masters, so must the modern religionist from his. Rather than decry it because, forsooth, we are such great biologists, let us go down on our knees to the past, and beg with all our prayers for one flash of its old radiant clear-seeing vision, its high calm wisdom, its stern duty, its loyal love.

O NE delusion indeed what we call the modern thirst for knowledge has engendered in us : that there is something new under the sun ; that our doubts and difficulties are new, and that our new teachers must find us new answers. The censors of modern literature are continually crying aloud for a new message. Where is the new prophet who will give peace to our souls? A very short time ago Browning's was the new message, Whitman's, Emerson's, Carlyle's, Ruskin's, Tennyson's. Was ever age more rich in prophets and in great messages? But what have we done with them ? Have we realised them in our lives, quite used up every available particle of their wisdom ? And yet here are we hungry and clamouring again. The truth is that the men who cry out for new messages mean rather new sensations of doubt. It is not peace they want, but fresh perplexity.

For peace is no new thing, any

more than perplexity. There is no quiddity of unbelief that is not to be found in mouldering parchments older than the religion of Christ. There is no assurance of faith that may ever be given us which has not long ago tranquillised the souls of forgotten saints. All the great men are of one mind. Their message is simple—so simple that we put it by. It seems so childish to our cultivated intelligences to say—Love God and love one another. The old prophets babbled that long ago. Yes, and the prophets to come will but repeat the same message in other forms. Truth always comes, as Christ came, in the garb of absolute simplicity. He seems a mere child or peasant person. The learned doctors will have none of Him. Love God and love one another! Is that all? That have we known from our youth up. Yet is there nothing else to say.

THE END

' BECAUSE thou hast seen Me, thou hast believed :
blessed are they that have not seen, and yet have
believed.'—ST. JOHN XX. 29.

' Blessed are the meek : for they shall inherit the
earth.'—ST. MATTHEW V. 5.

' This was thy daily task, *to learn that man
Is small, and not forget that man is great.*'
                      —A. C. BENSON.